The Quarter-Life Reset

The Quarter-Life Reset

Petchinsky

The Quarter-Life Reset: Thriving in Your 20s and 30s
By: Matthew Petchinsky

Introduction: Building the Foundation for Lifelong Success

Your 20s and 30s are often referred to as the "defining decades" of life—and for good reason. These pivotal years set the stage for the rest of your journey, providing the unique opportunity to lay down a foundation that will either propel you toward success or leave you scrambling to catch up later. While it's never too late to change course, understanding the importance of this time can help you make intentional, focused decisions that yield exponential benefits in your personal and professional life.

Why Your 20s and 30s Set the Stage for Success

The 20s and 30s are a time of discovery, experimentation, and growth. You're navigating the transition from adolescence to full adulthood, with all its challenges and opportunities. While this journey may feel overwhelming, these years offer incredible potential for creating a roadmap to success.

1. **Defining Identity and Purpose**

   In your 20s, you're faced with crucial questions about who you are and what you want out of life. These years are often marked by exploration—trying out different career paths, relationships, and lifestyles to figure out what resonates with you. By the time you enter your 30s, you're more likely to have a clearer sense of self, which allows you to make decisions aligned with your values and goals.

This period is about building the core of who you are. It's about discovering your passions and leveraging your unique strengths while learning from your failures. The choices you make during this time—whether it's pursuing further education, taking a career leap, or investing in meaningful relationships—set the tone for your personal and professional life.

2.Building Financial Security

Financial habits formed in your 20s and 30s often have a compounding effect on your future. These years provide the perfect window to learn about saving, investing, and budgeting. By making informed financial decisions early, you can avoid the pitfalls of debt and create a solid foundation for long-term stability.

Whether it's contributing to a retirement account, starting a side hustle, or building an emergency fund, the financial discipline you establish now pays off exponentially later. This isn't just about money—it's about freedom and the ability to take risks and seize opportunities without being held back by financial stress.

3.Career Momentum

Your professional trajectory often takes shape in your 20s and 30s. While it's natural to experiment with different roles early on, this is also the time to build skills, expand your network, and establish a reputation for excellence in your chosen field. These years offer the opportunity to lay the groundwork for promotions, partnerships, or entrepreneurial ventures that can define your career.

Each role, project, or challenge you take on is a stepping stone. Learning to adapt, lead, and innovate during this time builds the confidence and resilience needed for long-term career success.

4.Developing Relationships

Relationships formed during this stage of life can be some of the most meaningful and influential. Whether it's friendships, romantic partnerships, or professional connections, the people you surround yourself with have a profound impact on your growth. This is the time to cultivate relationships that uplift, challenge, and inspire you.

Networking becomes more than a buzzword; it becomes a critical tool for personal and professional development. The mentors, colleagues, and peers you connect with during this time can open doors to opportunities you may never have envisioned.

How to Reassess and Refocus

If you're reading this and feeling like you haven't made the most of your 20s or are uncertain about your 30s, don't worry—it's never too late to reassess and refocus. Success isn't about perfection; it's about intention and adaptation. Here's how to start:

1. **Take Inventory of Your Life**

   Reflect on where you are right now in terms of your career, finances, relationships, health, and personal growth. What's working? What's not? Be honest with yourself about your achievements and the areas where you've fallen short. This isn't about self-criticism; it's about self-awareness.

2. **Clarify Your Goals**

   Ask yourself: What do you want to achieve in the next five to ten years? Break those goals down into categories—career, financial, health, relationships, and personal fulfillment. Writing these down makes them tangible and provides a sense of direction.

3. **Identify Your Priorities**

   Not everything can be a priority at once. Focus on what matters most right now. This might mean accelerating your career, repairing a critical relationship, or building better financial habits. By prioritizing, you'll avoid the overwhelm of trying to tackle everything at once.

4. **Embrace the Power of Small Changes**

   Success often lies in the small, consistent habits we adopt. Whether it's dedicating 30 minutes a day to learning a new skill, exercising regularly, or setting aside a portion of your income for savings, incremental improvements create massive results over time.

5. **Seek Support and Accountability**

   Don't underestimate the power of mentors, coaches, and supportive friends. These individuals can provide guidance, encouragement, and constructive feedback as you navigate change.

Surround yourself with people who believe in your potential and hold you accountable for your progress.

6. **Be Flexible and Open to Change**

   Life rarely unfolds according to a rigid plan. Be willing to adapt, pivot, and try new approaches when something isn't working. Success isn't linear, and your ability to remain resilient and open-minded will determine how well you can navigate the challenges ahead.

The Journey Ahead

This book is your guide to making the most of your 20s and 30s, whether you're just starting out, reassessing your current trajectory, or looking to make a bold pivot. By understanding why these years are so important and learning how to refocus your efforts, you can create a future filled with purpose, stability, and success.

The journey begins now. It's time to step into your power and make the choices that will define not just the next decade but the rest of your life.

Chapter 1: Understanding Your Priorities

Life is a delicate balancing act, and the earlier you understand your priorities, the sooner you can direct your energy and resources toward what truly matters. Prioritization is the compass that guides you through the chaos of competing demands, helping you focus on the areas of life that align with your values, goals, and vision for the future. This chapter dives deep into the art and science of understanding your priorities, providing actionable insights and strategies to help you create a life centered around purpose and fulfillment.

The Foundation of Prioritization: Why It Matters

Prioritization is not just about managing time; it's about managing your life. Without clear priorities, it's easy to drift aimlessly, reacting to external demands rather than proactively shaping your journey. Misaligned priorities can lead to burnout, frustration, and regret as you expend energy on things that don't contribute to your long-term happiness or success.

Benefits of Understanding Your Priorities:

- **Clarity:** Knowing what matters most helps eliminate confusion and indecision.
- **Focus:** Prioritization keeps you centered on your goals, avoiding distractions.
- **Efficiency:** You can allocate your time, energy, and resources more effectively.
- **Fulfillment:** Living in alignment with your priorities leads to a more meaningful and satisfying life.

The Self-Assessment: Discovering What Truly Matters

Before you can set priorities, you need to understand yourself. This requires honest introspection to identify your core values, passions, and long-term goals.

1. **Identify Your Core Values**

   Your values are the principles that guide your decisions and actions. They reflect what's most important to you in life. Examples include integrity, family, personal growth, health, financial security, creativity, or contribution to society.

Exercise:

- ◦ Write down 10 values that resonate with you.
  ◦ Narrow the list to your top 3–5 values.
  ◦ Reflect on how these values show up in your daily life.

2.Define Your Passions

What activities or pursuits make you lose track of time? Understanding what excites and energizes you can help you align your priorities with your natural interests.

Questions to Ask Yourself:

- ◦ What brings me joy and fulfillment?
  ◦ What do I look forward to doing the most?
  ◦ What would I regret not pursuing?

3.Clarify Your Long-Term Goals

Goals provide direction and purpose. Consider where you want to be in the next 5, 10, or 20 years in key areas of life, such as career, health, relationships, and personal development.

Categories to Explore:

- ○ **Career:** What professional milestones do you want to achieve?
  ○ **Health:** How do you envision your physical and mental well-being?
  ○ **Relationships:** What kind of relationships do you want to nurture?
  ○ **Finances:** What financial goals are important to you?
  ○ **Personal Growth:** What skills, hobbies, or experiences do you want to develop?

The Priority Matrix: Organizing What Matters

Once you've identified what matters most, it's time to organize your priorities using a system that ensures you focus on the right things. One effective tool is the **Eisenhower Matrix**, which categorizes tasks and goals into four quadrants based on urgency and importance:

1. **Important and Urgent:** Tasks that require immediate attention (e.g., deadlines, emergencies).
2. **Important but Not Urgent:** High-value tasks that contribute to long-term goals (e.g., planning, learning new skills).
3. **Not Important but Urgent:** Tasks that may feel pressing but don't align with your priorities (e.g., unnecessary meetings).
4. **Not Important and Not Urgent:** Activities that waste time and energy (e.g., excessive social media scrolling).

Focus on Quadrants 1 and 2:

- Quadrant 1 ensures you handle immediate responsibilities.
- Quadrant 2 is where true growth and fulfillment happen, as you invest in long-term success.

Common Challenges in Prioritization and How to Overcome Them

Even with a clear understanding of your priorities, challenges will arise. Here's how to tackle them:

1. **Overcommitment**

   Saying "yes" to everything dilutes your focus. Learn to say "no" to requests that don't align with your priorities.

   Strategy: Use polite but firm responses, such as, "I appreciate the opportunity, but I need to focus on other commitments right now."

2. **Fear of Missing Out (FOMO)**

The fear of missing out can lead you to pursue things that aren't truly important to you.

Strategy: Remind yourself of your long-term goals and the trade-offs involved. Focus on what adds genuine value to your life.

3. **Procrastination**

Delaying important tasks can derail your priorities.

Strategy: Break tasks into smaller steps, set deadlines, and use tools like timers or accountability partners to stay on track.

4. **External Pressure**

Friends, family, or societal expectations may conflict with your priorities.

Strategy: Communicate your goals and boundaries clearly. Surround yourself with people who support your vision.

Creating an Action Plan for Priorities

Understanding your priorities is only the first step. You need to translate them into actionable plans.

Set SMART Goals:

Ensure your goals are Specific, Measurable, Achievable, Relevant, and Time-bound.

Example: Instead of saying, "I want to save money," say, "I will save $5,000 by the end of the year by cutting unnecessary expenses and increasing my income."

1. **Create a Daily Priority List:**
   Start each day by identifying your top 3 priorities. Ask yourself, "What's the most important thing I can accomplish today to move closer to my goals?"
2. **Use Time-Blocking:**
   Schedule dedicated time for your priorities. Treat these time blocks as non-negotiable appointments with yourself.
3. **Regularly Review and Adjust:**
   Life evolves, and so do your priorities. Set aside time every month to review your progress and make adjustments as needed.

Living in Alignment with Your Priorities

When your actions align with your priorities, you'll experience greater satisfaction and peace of mind. This alignment doesn't mean life will be free of challenges, but it does mean you'll face those challenges with a clear sense of purpose.

Understanding your priorities is a lifelong skill. As you grow and evolve, so will your goals and values. The key is to remain intentional, adaptable, and focused on what truly matters.

By mastering the art of prioritization, you'll not only achieve your goals but also build a life that reflects your deepest passions and values.

This foundation will serve as a springboard for everything you want to accomplish in the decades to come.

Chapter 2: Building Financial Confidence

Financial confidence is more than just knowing how to manage your money; it's about cultivating a mindset that empowers you to make informed, strategic decisions about your finances. This confidence acts as a safety net and springboard, helping you navigate challenges, seize opportunities, and create a future of stability and abundance. In this chapter, we'll explore the foundations of financial literacy, actionable steps to build financial confidence, and strategies for long-term wealth creation.

The Importance of Financial Confidence

Money is one of the most significant stressors for individuals, yet it's also one of the most powerful tools for achieving freedom and security. Financial confidence isn't about being wealthy—it's about having the knowledge, skills, and habits to manage your finances effectively, regardless of your income level.

Benefits of Financial Confidence:

- **Reduced Stress:** Understanding your finances minimizes anxiety about money.
- **Increased Opportunities:** With a clear financial picture, you can take calculated risks.
- **Empowerment:** Confidence in managing money leads to better decisions and control over your life.
- **Long-Term Security:** Building strong financial habits now sets you up for stability in the future.

The Foundations of Financial Literacy

Financial literacy is the cornerstone of financial confidence. To make empowered decisions, you must first understand key financial concepts.

1. **Budgeting:** The Blueprint of Your Financial Life
A budget is a plan for how you'll spend and save your money. It ensures that your income is allocated toward your needs, wants, and goals.

Key Steps to Create a Budget:

- ◦ **Track Your Expenses:** Monitor your spending for at least 30 days to understand where your money is going.
  ◦ **Categorize Spending:** Divide expenses into fixed (e.g., rent, utilities) and variable (e.g., dining out, entertainment).
  ◦ **Set Limits:** Assign a spending limit to each category based on your income and goals.
  ◦ **Adjust Regularly:** Review your budget monthly to reflect changes in income or expenses.

2.**Saving:** Preparing for the Future
Saving is the foundation of financial security. Whether it's for an emergency fund, a vacation, or retirement, setting aside money regularly ensures you're prepared for the expected and unexpected.

Savings Goals to Prioritize:

- ◦ **Emergency Fund:** Aim for 3–6 months' worth of living expenses.
  ◦ **Short-Term Goals:** Vacations, weddings, or big-ticket purchases.
  ◦ **Long-Term Goals:** Retirement, children's education, or buying a home.

Tips for Successful Saving:

- - Automate savings by setting up direct deposits into a separate account.
  - Start small and gradually increase the amount you save each month.

3.Debt Management: Gaining Control Over What You Owe
Debt isn't inherently bad, but unmanaged debt can quickly spiral out of control. Building financial confidence means understanding and managing your debt effectively.

Strategies for Managing Debt:

- - **Know Your Numbers:** List all debts, including balances, interest rates, and minimum payments.
  - **Prioritize High-Interest Debt:** Focus on paying off credit cards and other high-interest loans first.
  - **Consider the Snowball Method:** Pay off the smallest debts first to build momentum.
  - **Negotiate with Lenders:** Many lenders offer payment plans or reduced interest rates for proactive borrowers.

4.Investing: Growing Your Wealth

Investing allows your money to grow over time, creating wealth beyond what's possible through saving alone.

Basic Investing Concepts to Know:

- - **Compound Interest:** Your earnings generate their own earnings over time.
  - **Diversification:** Spread your investments across different asset classes to reduce risk.
  - **Risk Tolerance:** Understand your comfort level with investment risks based on your goals and timeline.

Types of Investments:

- - Stocks: Ownership in a company.
  - Bonds: Loans to corporations or governments with fixed returns.
  - Mutual Funds/ETFs: Pooled investments in a diversified portfolio.
  - Real Estate: Property investments for income or appreciation.

Developing Financial Confidence: Step-by-Step Guide

1. **Set Financial Goals:** Define your short-term, mid-term, and long-term goals.
   - **Short-Term:** Pay off $1,000 in debt within six months.
   - **Mid-Term:** Save for a down payment on a house in five years.
   - **Long-Term:** Retire with $1 million in investments by age 65.
2. **Educate Yourself:** Learn about money management and investing.
   - Read personal finance books, such as *The Total Money Makeover* by Dave Ramsey or *Rich Dad Poor Dad* by Robert Kiyosaki.
   - Follow trusted financial blogs or podcasts for practical advice.
3. **Build Good Habits:** Start small and focus on consistency.
   - Track expenses daily or weekly.
   - Automate bill payments and savings contributions.
   - Review your budget monthly and adjust as needed.
4. **Create a Financial Safety Net:**
   - Establish an emergency fund to cover unexpected expenses.
   - Get appropriate insurance (health, auto, home, and life) to protect against major financial risks.
5. **Monitor Your Progress:**
   - Use financial tracking apps or spreadsheets to see how your money is allocated.
   - Celebrate milestones, such as paying off a debt or reaching a savings goal.

Overcoming Common Financial Challenges

Even with a solid plan, financial obstacles are inevitable. Here's how to navigate them:

1. **Living Paycheck to Paycheck:**
   - **Solution:** Identify non-essential expenses to cut. Consider increasing income through side hustles or skills development.
2. **Impulse Spending:**
   - **Solution:** Delay purchases by 24–48 hours to evaluate necessity. Stick to a shopping list when making purchases.
3. **Fear of Investing:**
   - **Solution:** Start small with low-risk investments, such as index funds or robo-advisors. Learn as you go to build confidence.
4. **Unexpected Expenses:**
   - **Solution:** Build and maintain an emergency fund to avoid relying on credit.

The Mindset Shift: Confidence Comes from Action

Financial confidence isn't built overnight. It's the result of consistent action, learning from mistakes, and celebrating progress. Shift your mindset from fear and avoidance to empowerment and growth by adopting the following principles:

1. **Progress Over Perfection:** Focus on small, manageable improvements rather than aiming for flawless execution.
2. **Seek Help When Needed:** Consult financial advisors or mentors for guidance.
3. **Celebrate Wins:** Acknowledge milestones, no matter how small, to stay motivated.

Your Path to Financial Freedom

Building financial confidence is a journey that evolves over time. By mastering the basics of financial literacy, developing strong money habits, and maintaining a growth-oriented mindset, you'll set yourself up for a life of security and opportunity.

This chapter isn't just about numbers; it's about empowerment. With the tools and strategies provided here, you can take control of your financial future, transforming money from a source of stress into a foundation for success and freedom. The sooner you start, the greater your confidence will grow, creating ripple effects across every area of your life.

Chapter 3: Mastering the Art of Saying No

One of the most powerful tools for personal and professional success is the ability to say "no." While the word itself is simple, its implications are profound. Saying no allows you to protect your time, energy, and resources, ensuring that you stay focused on your priorities and values. Yet, for many people, saying no can feel uncomfortable or even impossible, especially when dealing with authority figures, loved ones, or societal expectations. In this chapter, we'll explore why saying no is essential, the psychology behind why it's so difficult, and actionable strategies to help you master this art with confidence and grace.

Why Saying No is Crucial for Success

In a world filled with endless demands and opportunities, saying yes to everything is a recipe for overwhelm, burnout, and mediocrity. Success isn't just about what you do—it's equally about what you choose not to do.

1. **Protects Your Time:** Time is your most valuable resource. Saying no ensures you have the bandwidth to focus on what truly matters.

2. **Maintains Focus on Priorities:** By declining distractions, you can dedicate your energy to your long-term goals and values.

3. **Prevents Burnout:** Overcommitting leads to exhaustion and diminished effectiveness. Saying no preserves your physical and mental health.

4. **Builds Self-Respect:** Setting boundaries reinforces your sense of self-worth and confidence.

5. **Enhances Quality of Work:** When you say no to tasks that dilute your focus, you can excel in the areas that matter most.

The Psychology of Saying No

Despite its importance, many people struggle with saying no due to psychological and emotional barriers. Understanding these barriers is the first step toward overcoming them.

1. **Fear of Conflict or Rejection:** Many people worry that saying no will upset others or damage relationships.
2. **Desire to Please:** A deeply ingrained need to be liked and accepted can make it hard to refuse requests.
3. **Guilt:** Turning someone down may evoke feelings of guilt, especially if you perceive their need as urgent or legitimate.
4. **FOMO (Fear of Missing Out):** Saying no to opportunities or invitations can feel like missing out on something valuable.
5. **Cultural or Social Conditioning:** Some cultures and communities emphasize selflessness, making it harder to prioritize personal needs.

The Costs of Always Saying Yes

Before delving into how to say no effectively, it's important to recognize the consequences of failing to set boundaries.

- **Overcommitment:** Leads to subpar performance and unmet expectations.
- **Stress and Anxiety:** Constantly trying to meet others' demands can take a toll on your mental health.
- **Loss of Identity:** Saying yes to everyone else's priorities can make you lose sight of your own.
- **Damaged Relationships:** Overextending yourself can lead to resentment, which strains relationships.

Strategies for Mastering the Art of Saying No

Saying no doesn't have to be confrontational or dismissive. With the right approach, you can decline requests while maintaining respect and kindness.

1. **Clarify Your Priorities:**
   Before you can confidently say no, you need to know what you're saying yes to. Understanding your goals and values helps you recognize when a request conflicts with them.

   Action Step: Write down your top three priorities and use them as a filter for decision-making.

   2.Adopt a Mindset Shift:

Saying no is not selfish—it's self-respect. Recognize that your time and energy are limited, and it's your responsibility to allocate them wisely.

Mantra to Remember: "Every time I say yes to something unimportant, I'm saying no to something that truly matters."

3.Use Polite and Direct Language:

Be firm but respectful when declining a request. You don't need to over-explain or justify your decision.

Examples of Phrases:

-
    - "Thank you for thinking of me, but I can't commit to this right now."
    - "I'm honored you asked, but I have other priorities at the moment."
    - "I appreciate the opportunity, but I'll have to pass this time."

4.Offer Alternatives (When Appropriate):

If you want to help but can't fulfill the request, suggest other resources or solutions.

Example:

-
    - "I can't take this on, but perhaps [another person or option] could help."

5.Practice the Pause:

If you're unsure about a request, buy time to evaluate whether it aligns with your priorities.

Response:

-
    - "Let me think about it and get back to you."

6.Set Clear Boundaries:
Proactively communicate your limits to prevent unnecessary requests.
Example:

- ◦ "I'm unavailable after 6 PM for work-related matters."

7.Reframe Your Perspective:
Remember that saying no is often better for both parties. Accepting a request you can't fulfill effectively doesn't help anyone.
Practical Scenarios and How to Say No

1. **Workplace Requests:**
   Scenario: A colleague asks you to take on extra tasks when your plate is already full.
   Response: "I'd love to help, but my current workload won't allow me to give this the attention it deserves. Have you spoken to [another colleague or supervisor] about this?"
2. **Social Invitations:**
   Scenario: A friend invites you to an event that doesn't align with your schedule or interests.
   Response: "Thank you for inviting me! I can't make it this time, but I'd love to catch up soon."
3. **Family Obligations:**
   Scenario: A family member expects you to handle a task you don't have the capacity for.
   Response: "I wish I could help, but I'm not able to right now. Maybe we can work on another solution together."
4. **Sales or Solicitations:**
   Scenario: Someone tries to sell you a product or service you're

not interested in.
Response: "Thank you for reaching out, but I'm not interested. Best of luck with your efforts!"

Overcoming the Guilt of Saying No
Feeling guilty after saying no is natural but unnecessary. Here's how to move past it:

1. **Remind Yourself of Your Why:** Focus on the priorities and values that informed your decision.
2. **Practice Self-Compassion:** Acknowledge that it's impossible to please everyone and that you're doing what's best for your well-being.
3. **Reframe the Situation:** Recognize that saying no allows others to find better-suited resources or solutions.

The Ripple Effect of Mastering No
As you become more confident in saying no, you'll notice profound changes in your life:

- **More Time for What Matters:** You'll have the bandwidth to focus on your goals and passions.
- **Improved Relationships:** Setting boundaries fosters mutual respect and healthier dynamics.
- **Greater Personal Fulfillment:** Living in alignment with your values brings deeper satisfaction.

A Lifelong Skill for Success
Mastering the art of saying no is a skill that will serve you throughout your life. It's not about being rigid or unkind—it's about honoring yourself and the commitments that matter most to you. By setting boundaries and declining with grace, you empower yourself to create a life filled with purpose, focus, and genuine success.

This chapter has equipped you with the tools to say no with confidence and clarity. As you move forward, remember: every no is a step toward a more intentional and fulfilling life.

Chapter 4: Developing Long-Term Habits

Habits are the building blocks of success. They shape your daily routines, influence your mindset, and ultimately determine the trajectory of your life. While short-term bursts of motivation can spark change, it's the habits you sustain over the long haul that lead to lasting transformation. This chapter explores the science of habit formation, how to design habits that align with your goals, and strategies to make them stick. By developing long-term habits, you'll create a foundation for a more focused, productive, and fulfilling life.

The Power of Habits

Habits are the automatic actions and decisions you make daily, often without conscious thought. They save mental energy by allowing your brain to operate on autopilot for routine behaviors. However, the cumulative effect of your habits—both positive and negative—can significantly impact your life.

1. **Why Habits Matter:**
   - **Compounding Effect:** Small, consistent actions lead to significant results over time.
   - **Efficiency:** Habits reduce decision fatigue by automating repetitive tasks.
   - **Identity Building:** The habits you adopt reflect and reinforce the person you want to become.
2. **Examples of Long-Term Habits:**
   - Positive: Exercising regularly, saving money, reading daily.
   - Negative: Procrastinating, overspending, neglecting health.

The Science of Habit Formation

Understanding how habits form is key to developing ones that last. The process of habit formation is often described using the **Habit Loop**, a three-step cycle identified by Charles Duhigg in *The Power of Habit*:

1. **Cue:** A trigger that initiates the habit (e.g., waking up in the morning).
2. **Routine:** The behavior itself (e.g., brushing your teeth).
3. **Reward:** The benefit or satisfaction you gain (e.g., fresh breath).

This cycle creates a feedback loop in your brain, strengthening the habit each time it's repeated.

How Long Does It Take to Form a Habit?

While the common belief is 21 days, research from the University College London suggests that it takes an average of **66 days** for a behavior to become automatic. The duration depends on the complexity of the habit and your consistency in practicing it.

Designing Habits That Stick

To develop habits that last, you need to design them intentionally. Here's a step-by-step guide:

1. **Start Small:**
   Begin with habits that are easy to integrate into your life. Small wins build momentum and confidence.

   Example: If you want to start exercising, begin with a 5-minute walk instead of a 30-minute workout.

2.**Be Specific:**
Clearly define your habit and the context in which it will occur.

   Example: Instead of saying, "I'll exercise more," say, "I'll go for a 15-minute walk every morning after breakfast."

3.**Anchor New Habits to Existing Ones:**
Use a habit you already do consistently as a trigger for a new habit. This technique is known as "habit stacking."

   Example: "After I brush my teeth in the morning, I'll spend 5 minutes meditating."

4.Make It Easy:

Remove barriers that make the habit difficult to perform. The less effort it takes, the more likely you are to follow through.

Example: Lay out your workout clothes the night before to make exercising in the morning seamless.

Focus on One Habit at a Time:

Trying to overhaul your life all at once is overwhelming. Prioritize one habit, master it, and then move on to the next.

Reinforcing Habits for the Long Term

Creating a habit is only half the battle. Maintaining it requires reinforcement and adaptability.

Track Your Progress:

Keeping a record of your habit can boost motivation and accountability. Use a habit tracker, journal, or app to log your efforts.

Example: Check off each day you complete your habit on a calendar.

Celebrate Small Wins:

Acknowledge and reward yourself for staying consistent, no matter how small the habit or milestone.

Example: Treat yourself to a favorite activity after completing a week of workouts.

1. **Anticipate Challenges:**

    Life will inevitably throw obstacles your way. Plan for setbacks and develop strategies to overcome them.

    Example: If you miss a workout, commit to resuming the next day instead of abandoning the habit entirely.

2.**Embrace the Power of Identity:**

Instead of focusing solely on the behavior, shift your mindset to adopt the identity of someone who performs the habit.

Example: Instead of saying, "I'm trying to run regularly," say, "I'm a runner."

The Role of Environment in Habit Formation

Your environment plays a significant role in shaping your habits. By designing a supportive environment, you make it easier to sustain positive habits and harder to fall into negative ones.

1. **Reduce Friction for Good Habits:**

    Make it convenient to perform your desired habits.

    Example: Keep healthy snacks visible and accessible to encourage better eating choices.

2. **Increase Friction for Bad Habits:**

Make undesirable behaviors more difficult to engage in.

Example: Remove junk food from your pantry to discourage mindless snacking.

3. **Surround Yourself with Support:**

The people around you influence your behavior. Spend time with individuals who share or encourage your habits.

Example: Join a workout group or find an accountability partner for fitness goals.

Breaking Bad Habits

While developing positive habits is essential, breaking negative ones is equally important. Here's how to tackle bad habits effectively:

1. **Identify Triggers:**
   Understand what cues the habit and work to eliminate or replace them.

   Example: If stress triggers overeating, find healthier stress-relief techniques like journaling or exercising.

2.**Substitute Positive Behaviors:**
Replace bad habits with healthier alternatives that fulfill the same need.
   Example: Instead of scrolling social media before bed, read a book to relax.

3.**Use the 20-Second Rule:**
Make it harder to engage in the bad habit by adding a 20-second delay.
   Example: Store your gaming console in a closet to reduce impulse gaming.

Building a Lifetime of Habits

Creating long-term habits is about consistency, not perfection. Focus on progress over time, and don't let occasional lapses derail your efforts.

1. **The Power of Kaizen:**
   Adopt the Japanese philosophy of continuous improvement. Even a 1% improvement each day compounds into massive growth over time.
2. **Reassess and Adapt:**
   As your goals and circumstances evolve, so should your habits. Periodically review your routines to ensure they still align with your priorities.
3. **Commit to Lifelong Learning:**
   Habits aren't static—they grow with you. Continuously seek ways to refine and optimize your routines.

Conclusion: Habits as the Blueprint for Success

Developing long-term habits is the key to achieving lasting success and fulfillment. By understanding the science of habit formation, designing habits that align with your goals, and reinforcing them consistently, you can create a life that reflects your highest potential.

Habits are more than just actions—they're expressions of your values, priorities, and identity. With intentionality and persistence, you can transform your daily routines into a powerful framework for personal and professional growth. Let this chapter serve as your guide to building the habits that will carry you toward a brighter and more purposeful future.

Chapter 5: Planning for Your Future Success

Success rarely happens by accident. It is the result of clear, strategic planning, combined with consistent effort and adaptability. Planning for your future success involves setting meaningful goals, creating actionable steps, and maintaining a vision of where you want to go. In this chapter, we'll explore the importance of planning, provide frameworks for setting and achieving goals, and offer practical strategies for staying on track. By the end of this chapter, you'll have the tools to design a roadmap to a future filled with purpose, growth, and achievement.

Why Planning is Essential for Success

Planning is the bridge between where you are now and where you want to be. Without a plan, even the most ambitious goals can remain out of reach. A well-thought-out plan provides clarity, direction, and motivation, making it easier to navigate challenges and measure progress.

The Benefits of Planning:

1. **Clarity of Purpose:** Knowing your goals helps you prioritize your time and energy.
2. **Increased Productivity:** A plan helps you focus on high-value tasks that move you closer to success.
3. **Reduced Stress:** Having a roadmap minimizes uncertainty and allows you to take proactive steps.
4. **Accountability:** Tracking progress ensures you stay committed to your goals.
5. **Adaptability:** A plan provides a framework for adjusting when circumstances change.

Step 1: Define Your Vision

Before you can create a plan, you need a clear vision of what success looks like for you. Your vision serves as your North Star, guiding your decisions and actions.

1. **Visualize Your Ideal Future:**

   Imagine yourself 5, 10, or 20 years from now. Consider:
   - What does your ideal career look like?
   - What kind of relationships do you have?
   - What level of financial security have you achieved?
   - What personal achievements or experiences have you accomplished?

Exercise:

Write a detailed description of your ideal life. Include specifics about your career, health, finances, relationships, and personal growth.

1. **Identify Core Values:**

   Align your vision with your values to ensure it reflects what truly matters to you.

2. **Set Long-Term Goals:**

   Break your vision into specific, measurable goals. These goals should cover key areas of your life, such as:
   - **Career:** Achieving a leadership position, starting a business, or transitioning to a fulfilling role.
   - **Health:** Maintaining physical fitness, achieving mental wellness, or adopting healthy habits.
   - **Finances:** Building wealth, paying off debt, or saving for retirement.

- ◦ **Personal Growth:** Learning new skills, pursuing hobbies, or contributing to your community.

Step 2: Break Goals Into Actionable Steps

Large goals can feel overwhelming, but breaking them into smaller, actionable steps makes them manageable and achievable.

1. **SMART Goals Framework:**

   Ensure your goals are:
   - ◦ **Specific:** Clearly define what you want to achieve.
   - ◦ **Measurable:** Establish criteria for tracking progress.
   - ◦ **Achievable:** Set realistic goals that stretch you without being unattainable.
   - ◦ **Relevant:** Align goals with your values and priorities.
   - ◦ **Time-Bound:** Set deadlines to create urgency.

Example of a SMART Goal:

Instead of "Save money," say, "Save $5,000 for an emergency fund by December 31 by setting aside $500 monthly."

2. **Create Milestones:**

Divide long-term goals into smaller milestones to maintain momentum.

Example: If your goal is to run a marathon in a year, milestones might include:

- ◦ Month 1: Run 5 miles consistently.
- ◦ Month 6: Complete a half-marathon.
- ◦ Month 12: Achieve full marathon readiness.

3.Prioritize Tasks:

Focus on tasks that provide the highest return on investment for your time and energy. Use tools like the Eisenhower Matrix to prioritize effectively.

Step 3: Develop a Timeline and Action Plan

A timeline transforms your goals into a structured plan of action.

1. **Set Deadlines:** Assign deadlines to each milestone and task to maintain accountability.
2. **Use Time-Blocking:** Allocate specific time slots in your schedule for goal-related activities.
3. **Leverage Tools and Resources:** Use planners, calendars, or project management apps (e.g., Trello, Asana) to organize tasks and deadlines.

Example Timeline for Starting a Business:

- **Month 1:** Conduct market research and finalize your business idea.
- **Month 2:** Develop a business plan and secure funding.
- **Month 3:** Launch your product or service and begin marketing.

Step 4: Overcome Obstacles and Stay Consistent

Even the best plans encounter roadblocks. Anticipating and addressing challenges is critical to staying on course.

Identify Potential Obstacles:

Consider what might hinder your progress and develop contingency plans.

Example: If lack of time is a challenge, identify areas where you can delegate or eliminate non-essential tasks.

1. **Build Resilience:**
   Adopt a growth mindset, viewing setbacks as opportunities to learn and adapt.
2. **Establish Accountability:**
   Share your goals with a trusted friend, mentor, or coach who can provide encouragement and hold you accountable.
3. **Track and Reflect on Progress:**
   Regularly review your plan and assess your progress. Use metrics to measure success and make adjustments as needed.

Reflection Questions:

- ○ What's working well?
  ○ What needs to change?
  ○ Are your goals still aligned with your vision?

Step 5: Adapt and Evolve

Life is dynamic, and your goals may shift as circumstances change. Flexibility is key to long-term success.

1. **Revisit Your Vision:**

   Periodically reflect on your vision to ensure it aligns with your current values and aspirations.

2. **Embrace Change:**

   Recognize that changing a goal isn't failure—it's growth. Adapt your plan to reflect new opportunities or priorities.

3. **Celebrate Wins:**

   Acknowledge and reward yourself for achieving milestones, no matter how small. Celebrating progress keeps you motivated and reinforces positive behavior.

Practical Tools for Future Planning

1. **Vision Boards:**

   Create a visual representation of your goals and aspirations to stay inspired.

2. **Journaling:**

   Write regularly about your progress, insights, and challenges. This practice fosters self-awareness and clarity.

3. **Mind Mapping:**

   Use mind maps to brainstorm and organize your goals and action steps.

4. **Financial Planning:**

   Work with a financial advisor or use budgeting apps to ensure your financial goals align with your broader vision.

The Role of Mindset in Future Planning

Planning for success isn't just about strategy—it's also about mindset. Cultivate a positive, growth-oriented attitude to overcome challenges and maintain momentum.

1. **Visualize Success:**
   Spend time imagining yourself achieving your goals. This mental rehearsal builds confidence and motivation.
2. **Practice Gratitude:**
   Focus on what you've accomplished and the opportunities ahead. Gratitude fosters resilience and a sense of abundance.
3. **Stay Curious:**
   Approach your journey with curiosity and a willingness to learn. Adaptability is a hallmark of successful planning.

Conclusion: Designing Your Path to Success

Planning for your future success is an investment in yourself and your dreams. By defining your vision, setting clear goals, and creating actionable plans, you can take control of your life's direction. Remember, success is a journey, not a destination. The process of planning, adapting, and growing is as valuable as the achievements themselves.

With the strategies in this chapter, you have the tools to design a future filled with purpose, accomplishment, and fulfillment. Your success starts with the plans you make today—so take that first step and begin building the life you've always envisioned.

Appendix A: Goal-Setting Templates and Financial Tracking Tools

To complement the strategies and insights shared in this book, this appendix provides practical templates and tools to help you implement your plans effectively. These resources are designed to simplify the processes of goal setting and financial tracking, ensuring that you have a clear and organized approach to achieving your dreams.

Goal-Setting Templates

The following templates will help you break down your vision into actionable and measurable steps. Customize these templates to fit your personal and professional goals.

1. SMART Goals Template

Use this template to define your goals using the SMART criteria: Specific, Measurable, Achievable, Relevant, and Time-bound.

Category	Details
Goal Name	Write a concise name for your goal.
Specific	What exactly do you want to achieve? Be clear and detailed.
Measurable	How will you measure progress? Define metrics or milestones.
Achievable	Is this goal realistic? If not, what adjustments can make it achievable?
Relevant	Why is this goal important to you? How does it align with your values and long-term vision?

Category	Details
Time-bound	What is your deadline? Set a clear time frame for completion.

Example:

- **Goal Name:** Build an Emergency Fund
- **Specific:** Save $5,000 for emergencies.
- **Measurable:** Save $500 per month.
- **Achievable:** Reduce discretionary spending and increase income with a side hustle.
- **Relevant:** Financial security is essential for reducing stress and achieving independence.
- **Time-bound:** Complete savings goal by December 31, 2025.

2. Weekly Goal Tracker

This tool helps you monitor short-term progress on a weekly basis, keeping you accountable and motivated.

Week	Goal	Action Steps	Progress	Next Steps
Week 1	Goal description	List 2–3 specific actions.	Percent completed.	What to do next week.
Example: Save $100	Reduce dining out	Bring lunch to work, skip coffee shops.	80% (Saved $80)	Adjust spending plan to save the rest.

3. Milestone Mapping Template

This template is ideal for breaking down long-term goals into smaller, manageable milestones.

Long-Term Goal	Target Completion Date	Milestones	Deadline for Milestone	Progress
Example: Publish a book	Dec. 31, 2025	Outline chapters	Mar. 31, 2025	In progress
		Complete manuscript	Aug. 31, 2025	Not started
		Secure editor and finalize	Nov. 30, 2025	Not started

Financial Tracking Tools

Financial tracking is essential for understanding your current situation, monitoring progress, and making informed decisions. Use the tools below to stay organized and disciplined in managing your finances.

1. Monthly Budget Template

Track your income and expenses with this simple monthly budget template to ensure your spending aligns with your financial goals.

Category	Planned Amount	Actual Amount	Difference
Income			
Salary	$	$	$
Side Hustles	$	$	$
Other Income	$	$	$
Total Income	$	$	$
Expenses			
Rent/Mortgage	$	$	$
Utilities	$	$	$
Transportation	$	$	$
Groceries	$	$	$
Dining Out	$	$	$

Category	Planned Amount	Actual Amount	Difference
Entertainment	$	$	$
Savings	$	$	$
Debt Payments	$	$	$
Total Expenses	$	$	$
Net Income	(Income - Expenses)	$	$

2. Debt Repayment Tracker

Use this tool to create a clear plan for paying off debts, prioritizing high-interest debts first or using the debt snowball method.

Debt Name	Balance	Interest Rate	Minimum Payment	Extra Payment	Progress
Credit Card 1	$	%	$	$	%
Credit Card 2	$	%	$	$	%
Student Loan	$	%	$	$	%
Car Loan	$	%	$	$	%

3. Savings Tracker

Monitor your progress toward specific savings goals, whether for an emergency fund, a vacation, or a major purchase.

Savings Goal	Target Amount	Monthly Contribution	Start Date	Target Completion Date	Progress
Emergency Fund	$	$	MM/DD/YYYY	MM/DD/YYYY	%
Vacation	$	$	MM/DD/YYYY	MM/DD/YYYY	%
Home Down Payment	$	$	MM/DD/YYYY	MM/DD/YYYY	%

4. Net Worth Calculator

Track your overall financial health by calculating your net worth—your assets minus your liabilities.

Assets	Value	Liabilities	Value
Cash Savings	$	Credit Card Debt	$
Investment Accounts	$	Student Loans	$
Real Estate	$	Car Loan	$
Other Assets	$	Other Liabilities	$
Total Assets	$	**Total Liabilities**	$
Net Worth	(Assets - Liabilities)	$	

Tips for Using These Templates and Tools

1. **Be Consistent:** Regularly update your templates and trackers to maintain an accurate picture of your progress.
2. **Set Reminders:** Schedule weekly or monthly check-ins to review your goals and finances.
3. **Stay Flexible:** Adjust your plans as needed to reflect changes in circumstances or priorities.
4. **Celebrate Milestones:** Recognize and reward yourself for achieving significant goals.

Conclusion

This appendix provides a practical toolkit to support your journey toward success. By using these templates and tracking tools, you'll gain greater clarity, organization, and control over your goals and finances. Remember, success is not just about dreaming big—it's about breaking those dreams into actionable steps and tracking your progress every step of the way.

<u>Message from the Author:</u>

I hope you enjoyed this book, I love astrology and knew there was not a book such as this out on the shelf. I love metaphysical items as well. Please check out my other books:

-Life of Government Benefits

-My life of Hell

-My life with Hydrocephalus

-Red Sky

-World Domination:Woman's rule

-World Domination:Woman's Rule 2: The War

-Life and Banishment of Apophis: book 1

-The Kidney Friendly Diet

-The Ultimate Hemp Cookbook

-Creating a Dispensary(legally)

-Cleanliness throughout life: the importance of showering from childhood to adulthood.

-Strong Roots: The Risks of Overcoddling children

-Hemp Horoscopes: Cosmic Insights and Earthly Healing

- Celestial Hemp Navigating the Zodiac: Through the Green Cosmos

-Astrological Hemp: Aligning The Stars with Earth's Ancient Herb

-The Astrological Guide to Hemp: Stars, Signs, and Sacred Leaves

-Green Growth: Innovative Marketing Strategies for your Hemp Products and Dispensary

-Cosmic Cannabis

-Astrological Munchies

-Henry The Hemp

-Zodiacal Roots: The Astrological Soul Of Hemp

- **Green Constellations: Intersection of Hemp and Zodiac**

-Hemp in The Houses: An astrological Adventure Through The Cannabis Galaxy

-Galactic Ganja Guide

Heavenly Hemp

Zodiac Leaves

Doctor Who Astrology

Cannastrology

Stellar Satvias and Cosmic Indicas

<u>Celestial Cannabis: A Zodiac Journey</u>

AstroHerbology: The Sky and The Soil: Volume 1

AstroHerbology:Celestial Cannabis:Volume 2

Cosmic Cannabis Cultivation

The Starry Guide to Herbal Harmony: Volume 1

The Starry Guide to Herbal Harmony: Cannabis Universe: Volume 2

Yugioh Astrology: Astrological Guide to Deck, Duels and more

Nightmare Mansion: Echoes of The Abyss

Nightmare Mansion 2: Legacy of Shadows

Nightmare Mansion 3: Shadows of the Forgotten

Nightmare Mansion 4: Echoes of the Damned

The Life and Banishment of Apophis: Book 2

Nightmare Mansion: Halls of Despair

<u>Healing with Herb: Cannabis and Hydrocephalus</u>

<u>Planetary Pot: Aligning with Astrological Herbs: Volume 1</u>

Fast Track to Freedom: 30 Days to Financial Independence Using AI, Assets, and Agile Hustles

<u>Cosmic Hemp Pathways</u>

How to Become Financially Free in 30 Days: 10,000 Paths to Prosperity

Zodiacal Herbage: Astrological Insights: Volume 1

Nightmare Mansion: Whispers in the Walls

The Daleks Invade Atlantis

Henry the hemp and Hydrocephalus

10X The Kidney Friendly Diet

Cannabis Universe: Adult coloring book

Hemp Astrology: The Healing Power of the Stars

Zodiacal Herbage: Astrological Insights: Cannabis Universe: Volume 2

<u>Planetary Pot: Aligning with Astrological Herbs: Cannabis Universes: Volume 2</u>

Doctor Who Meets the Replicators and SG-1: The Ultimate Battle for Survival

Nightmare Mansion: Curse of the Blood Moon

<u>The Celestial Stoner: A Guide to the Zodiac</u>

Cosmic Pleasures: Sex Toy Astrology for Every Sign

Hydrocephalus Astrology: Navigating the Stars and Healing Waters

Lapis and the Mischievous Chocolate Bar

Celestial Positions: Sexual Astrology for Every Sign

Apophis's Shadow Work Journal: **:** A Journey of Self-Discovery and Healing

Kinky Cosmos: Sexual Kink Astrology for Every Sign

Digital Cosmos: The Astrological Digimon Compendium

Stellar Seeds: The Cosmic Guide to Growing with Astrology

Apophis's Daily Gratitude Journal

Cat Astrology: Feline Mysteries of the Cosmos

The Cosmic Kama Sutra: An Astrological Guide to Sexual Positions

Unleash Your Potential: A Guided Journal Powered by AI Insights

Whispers of the Enchanted Grove

Cosmic Pleasures: An Astrological Guide to Sexual Kinks

369, 12 Manifestation Journal

Whisper of the nocturne journal(blank journal for writing or drawing)

The Boogey Book

Locked In Reflection: A Chastity Journey Through Locktober

Generating Wealth Quickly:

How to Generate $100,000 in 24 Hours

Star Magic: Harness the Power of the Universe

The Flatulence Chronicles: A Fart Journal for Self-Discovery

The Doctor and The Death Moth

Seize the Day: A Personal Seizure Tracking Journal

The Ultimate Boogeyman Safari: A Journey into the Boogie World and Beyond

Whispers of Samhain: 1,000 Spells of Love, Luck, and Lunar Magic: Samhain Spell Book

Apophis's guides:

Witch's Spellbook Crafting Guide for Halloween

<u>Frost & Flame: The Enchanted Yule Grimoire of 1000 Winter Spells</u>

<u>The Ultimate Boogey Goo Guide & Spooky Activities for Halloween Fun</u>

Harmony of the Scales: A Libra's Spellcraft for Balance and Beauty

The Enchanted Advent: 36 Days of Christmas Wonders

Nightmare Mansion: The Labyrinth of Screams

Harvest of Enchantment: 1,000 Spells of Gratitude, Love, and Fortune for Thanksgiving

The Boogey Chronicles: A Journal of Nightly Encounters and Shadowy Secrets

The 12 Days of Financial Freedom: A Step-by-Step Christmas Countdown to Transform Your Finances

Sigil of the Eternal Spiral Blank Journal

A Christmas Feast: Timeless Recipes for Every Meal

Cosmic Sales: The Astrological Guide to Black Friday Shopping
Legends of the Corn Mother and Other Harvest Myths
Whispers of the Harvest: The Corn Mother's Journal
The Evergreen Spellbook
The Doctor Meets the Boogeyman
The White Witch of Rose Hall's SpellBook
The Gingerbread Golem's Shadow: A Study in Sweet Darkness
The Gingerbread Golem Codex: An Academic Exploration of Sweet Myths
The Gingerbread Golem Grimoire: Sweet Magicks and Spells for the Festive Witch
The Curse of the Gingerbread Golem
10-minute Christmas Crafts for kids
<u>Christmas Crisis Solutions: The Ultimate Last-Minute Survival Guide</u>
Gingerbread Golem Recipes: Holiday Treats with a Magical Twist
The Infinite Key: Unlocking Mystical Secrets of the Ages
Enchanted Yule: A Wiccan and Pagan Guide to a Magical and Memorable Season
Dinosaurs of Power: Unlocking Ancient Magick
Astro-Dinos: The Cosmic Guide to Prehistoric Wisdom
Gallifrey's Yule Logs: A Festive Doctor Who Cookbook
The Dino Grimoire: Secrets of Prehistoric Magick
The Gift They Never Knew They Needed
The Gingerbread Golem's Culinary Alchemy: Enchanting Recipes for a Sweetly Dark Feast
A Time Lord Christmas: Holiday Adventures with the Doctor
Krampusproofing Your Home: Defensive Strategies for Yule
Silent Frights: A Collection of Christmas Creepypastas to Chill Your Bones
Santa Raptor's Jolly Carnage: A Dino-Claus Christmas Tale
Prehistoric Palettes: A Dino Wicca Coloring Journey
The Christmas Wishkeeper Chronicles

If you want solar for your home go here: https://www.harborso-lar.live/apophisenterprises/

Get Some Tarot cards: https://www.makeplayingcards.com/sell/apophis-occult-shop

Get   some   shirts: https://www.bonfire.com/store/apophis-shirt-emporium/

<u>Instagrams:</u>
@apophis_enterprises,
@apophisbookemporium,
@apophisscardshop
Twitter: @apophisenterpr1
Tiktok:@apophisenterprise
Youtube: @sg1fan23477, @FiresideRetreatKingdom
Hive: @sg1fan23477
CheeLee: @SG1fan23477

Podcast: Apophis Chat Zone: https://open.spotify.com/show/5zXbrCLEV2xzCp8ybrfHsk?si=fb4d4fdbdce44dec

Newsletter: https://apophiss-newsletter-27c897.beehiiv.com/

If you want to support me or see posts of other projects that I have come over to: **buymeacoffee.com/mpetchinskg**
I post there daily several times a day

Get your Dinowicca or Christmas themed digital products, especially Santa Raptor songs and other musics. Here: **https://sg1fan23477.gumroad.com**

Apophis Yuletide Digital has not only digital Christmas items, but it will have all things with Dinowicca as well as other Digital products.